This journal belongs to

_____

DEPARTE
02 SEP 20
HONG

Belle City Gifts
Racine, Wisconsin, USA

Belle City Gifts is an imprint of BroadStreet Publishing Group LLC.
Broadstreetpublishing.com

The Lord Your God Is With You

ISBN 978-1-4245-5486-7

Design by Garborg Design Works | garborgdesign.com
Compiled and edited by Michelle Winger | literallyprecise.com

Printed in China.

17 18 19 20 21 22 23   7 6 5 4 3 2 1

Introduction

Our world is so big that even if we traveled every day of our lives we'd never see it all. There would still be lagoons to snorkel, mountains to crest, and hidden nooks and crannies of creation to explore. To those of us afflicted with wanderlust, the possibilities seem limitless.

And still we get bored. Right under our noses there are buds beginning to bloom, leaves preparing to fall, lizards scurrying over rocks, or tiny ants carrying tremendous loads. Above us there's a sky filled with so many distant worlds that our minds cannot fathom its expanse.

Today, wherever the road takes you, open your eyes. Instead of hurrying past what you've already seen, look again. Take time to appreciate the detail God has woven into the world around you.

Take delight in the LORD,
and he will give you your heart's desires.
Commit everything you do to the LORD.
Trust him, and he will help you.

PSALM 37:4-5 NLT

_____

_____

_____

_____

_____

_____

_____

_____

_____

_____

_____

_____

_____

_____

_____

_____

_____

_____

_____

_____

_____

_____

_____

_____

_____

_____

_____

_____

_____

_____

_____

_____

_____

_____

_____

_____

_____

_____

_____

_____

_____

Today, wherever the road takes you, open
your eyes. Instead of hurrying past
what you've already seen, look again.
Take time to appreciate the detail
God has woven into nature.

I will declare that your love stands firm forever,
that you have established your faithfulness in heaven itself.

PSALM 89:2 NIV

_____

_____

_____

_____

_____

_____

_____

_____

_____

_____

_____

_____

_____

_____

_____

_____

_____

_____

_____

_____

_____

Make the most of moments
with loved ones today.

Be my rock of refuge,
to which I can always go;
give the command to save me,
for you are my rock and my fortress.

PSALM 71:3 NIV

_____

_____

_____

_____

_____

_____

_____

_____

_____

_____

_____

_____

_____

_____

_____

_____

_____

_____

There's so much more to this life
than what we can see with our eyes.

Consider it pure joy, my brothers and sisters, whenever you face trials of many kinds, because you know that the testing of your faith produces perseverance.

JAMES 1:2-3 NIV

_____

_____

_____

_____

_____

_____

_____

_____

_____

_____

_____

_____

_____

_____

_____

_____

_____

_____

_____

_____

_____

_____

_____

_____

_____

_____

_____

_____

_____

_____

_____

_____

_____

_____

_____

_____

_____

_____

_____

_____

God's world is like a treasure map pointing us right back to him. All we have to do is follow the clues.

My child, pay attention to what I say.
Listen carefully to my words.
Don't lose sight of them.

PROVERBS 4:20-21 NLT

Let awe find a permanent home
in your heart.

Momentary, light affliction is producing for us an eternal weight of glory far beyond all comparison.

2 CORINTHIANS 4:17 NASB

_____

_____

_____

_____

_____

_____

_____

_____

_____

_____

_____

_____

_____

_____

_____

_____

_____

_____

_____

_____

God's greatest masterpiece
can be found in a mirror.

At each and every sunrise you will hear my voice
as I prepare my sacrifice of prayer to you.
Every morning I lay out the pieces of my life on the altar
and wait for your fire to fall upon my heart.

PSALM 5:3 TPT

_____

_____

_____

_____

_____

_____

_____

_____

_____

_____

_____

_____

_____

_____

_____

_____

_____

_____

_____

_____

At sunrise and sunset, God paints the sky
with color, light, and creativity.

Let the message about Christ, in all its richness, fill your lives. Sing psalms and hymns and spiritual songs to God with thankful hearts.

COLOSSIANS 3:16 NLT

_____

_____

_____

_____

_____

_____

_____

_____

_____

_____

_____

_____

_____

_____

_____

_____

_____

_____

_____

_____

_____

_____

_____

_____

_____

_____

_____

_____

_____

_____

_____

_____

_____

_____

_____

_____

_____

_____

_____

_____

Time we've set aside to relax isn't a critical task we're required to accomplish. It's a gift to be opened leisurely and enjoyed.

Let [my words] penetrate deep into your heart,
for they bring life to those who find them,
and healing to their whole body.

PROVERBS 4:21-22 NLT

_____

_____

_____

_____

_____

_____

_____

_____

_____

_____

_____

_____

_____

_____

_____

_____

_____

_____

_____

Grab hold of the here-and-now,
and savor every moment.

I walk in the way of righteousness,
along the paths of justice,
bestowing a rich inheritance on those who love me
and making their treasuries full.

PROVERBS 8:20-21 NIV

_____

_____

_____

_____

_____

_____

_____

_____

_____

_____

_____

_____

_____

_____

_____

_____

_____

_____

_____

_____

_____

_____

Enjoying a little R & R is not a waste of time.
It's one way of following God's example of rest.

Above all, clothe yourselves with love,
which binds us all together in perfect harmony.

COLOSSIANS 3:14 NLT

_____

_____

_____

_____

_____

_____

_____

_____

_____

_____

_____

_____

_____

_____

_____

_____

_____

_____

_____

_____

_____

_____

_____

The more frequently you clothe yourself
in God's couture, the more difficult
it becomes to remove it.

Be patient with each other, making allowance for each other's faults because of your love.

EPHESIANS 4:2 NLT

_____

_____

_____

_____

_____

_____

_____

_____

_____

_____

_____

_____

_____

_____

_____

_____

_____

_____

_____

No exotic location could ever provide the joy
we find in the presence of those we love.

"Let your light shine before others, so that they may see your good works and give glory to your Father who is in heaven."

MATTHEW 5:16 ESV

_____

_____

_____

_____

_____

_____

_____

_____

_____

_____

_____

_____

_____

_____

_____

_____

_____

_____

_____

_____

_____

If God's ultimate purpose is that we love him
and love others, we need to temper our **me**
time with **we** time.

The God of gods, the mighty Lord himself, has spoken!
He shouts out over all the people of the earth,
In every brilliant sunrise and every beautiful sunset, saying,
"Listen to me!"

PSALM 50:1 TPT

_____

_____

_____

_____

_____

_____

_____

_____

_____

_____

_____

_____

_____

_____

_____

_____

_____

_____

_____

_____

Learning is not at odds with relaxation.
It can spark new interests, challenge us to
rethink long-held opinions, and stir up some
interesting conversations.

Be still, and know that I am God;
I will be exalted among the nations,
I will be exalted in the earth!

PSALM 46:10 NKJV

_____
_____
_____
_____
_____
_____
_____
_____
_____
_____
_____
_____
_____
_____
_____
_____
_____
_____
_____
_____

_____

_____

_____

_____

_____

_____

_____

_____

_____

_____

_____

_____

_____

_____

_____

_____

_____

_____

_____

_____

_____

_____

_____

Happy memories are a great souvenir. They're free, easy to carry, and never need dusting.

Let the sea and everything in it shout his praise!
Let the earth and all living things join in.

PSALM 98:7 NLT

_____

_____

_____

_____

_____

_____

_____

_____

_____

_____

_____

_____

_____

_____

_____

_____

_____

_____

_____

_____

_____

_____

_____

_____

_____

_____

_____

_____

_____

_____

_____

_____

_____

_____

_____

_____

_____

_____

_____

_____

_____

_____

_____

On vacation days, we often experience
situations that will put our patience,
preconceived notions, and unconditional
love to the test. These days provide the perfect
petri dish in which faith can grow!

I lie awake at night thinking of you—of how much you have helped me—
and how I rejoice through the night beneath the protecting shadow
of your wings.

PSALM 63:6-7 TLB

_____

_____

_____

_____

_____

_____

_____

_____

_____

_____

_____

_____

_____

_____

_____

_____

_____

_____

*There's no better time than today to begin a
practice of quietness that helps us enjoy the
beauty of the moment and invites us to draw
closer to God at the same time.*

Don't be pulled in different directions or worried about a thing.
Be saturated in prayer throughout each day, offering your faith-filled
requests before God with overflowing gratitude.

PHILIPPIANS 4:6 TPT

_____

_____

_____

_____

_____

_____

_____

_____

_____

_____

_____

_____

_____

_____

_____

_____

_____

_____

_____

To be a Christian without prayer is no more
possible than to be alive without breathing. –
Martin Luther

The earth is the LORD's, and everything in it,
the world, and all who live in it.

PSALM 24:1 NIV

_____

_____

_____

_____

_____

_____

_____

_____

_____

_____

_____

_____

_____

_____

_____

_____

_____

_____

_____

God designed us for relationship; we are
children created to love and be loved.

We can make our plans, but the final outcome is in God's hands.

PROVERBS 16:1 TLB

_____

_____

_____

_____

_____

_____

_____

_____

_____

_____

_____

_____

_____

_____

_____

_____

_____

_____

_____

_____

_____

_____

_____

_____

_____

_____

_____

_____

_____

_____

_____

_____

_____

_____

_____

_____

_____

_____

_____

_____

_____

_____

We may believe the purpose of our vacation is to see the world, but God may have an even richer purpose in mind.

On the seventh day God had finished his work of creation,
so he rested from all his work.

GENESIS 2:2 NLT

_____

_____

_____

_____

_____

_____

_____

_____

_____

_____

_____

_____

_____

_____

_____

_____

_____

_____

_____

Play time is as important for adults as it is for kids. We need time to laugh, to explore, to create, to try new things, to dream. We need to give ourselves permission to allow the child in us to come out and play.

Then you will go on your way in safety,
and your foot will not stumble.
When you lie down, you will not be afraid;
when you lie down, your sleep will be sweet.

PROVERBS 3:23-24 NIV

_____

_____

_____

_____

_____

_____

_____

_____

_____

_____

_____

_____

_____

_____

_____

_____

_____

_____

_____

_____

_____

Travel can weave a crazy quilt of emotions
inside us. The one that should overwhelm us
again and again is gratitude.

The steadfast love of the LORD never ceases;
his mercies never come to an end;
they are new every morning;
great is your faithfulness.

LAMENTATIONS 3:22-23 ESV

_____

_____

_____

_____

_____

_____

_____

_____

_____

_____

_____

_____

_____

_____

_____

_____

_____

_____

_____

_____

_____

_____

_____

_____

_____

_____

_____

_____

_____

_____

_____

_____

_____

_____

_____

_____

_____

Having enough to eat—or more than enough—
is not a given. It is a gift. Taking time to
thank God for what's on our plate—whether it's
samosas, kimchi, or pickled pigs' feet—reminds
us that food is first and foremost fuel. Taste is
an added bonus.

You saw me before I was born.
Every day of my life was recorded in your book.
Every moment was laid out
before a single day had passed.

PSALM 139:16 NLT

_____

_____

_____

_____

_____

_____

_____

_____

_____

_____

_____

_____

_____

_____

_____

_____

_____

_____

_____

_____

Happy memories are an irreplaceable gift.

We travel not to escape life,
but for life not to escape us.

> "If only I could fly away from all of this!
> If only I could run away to the place of rest and peace.
> I would run far away where no one could find me,
> Escaping to a wilderness retreat."
>
> PSALM 55:6-7 TPT

_____

_____

_____

_____

_____

_____

_____

_____

_____

_____

_____

_____

_____

_____

_____

_____

_____

_____

_____

_____

_____

How beautiful it is to do nothing
and then rest afterwards.

When we obey him, every path he guides us on is fragrant with his loving-kindness and his truth.

PSALM 25:10 TLB

_____

_____

_____

_____

_____

_____

_____

_____

_____

_____

_____

_____

_____

_____

_____

_____

_____

_____

Wherever today finds you, you're surrounded by God's handiwork. Every landscape, every wildflower, every face that you see can remind you of him—and provide a clue about the character of his divine nature.

This is the day the LORD has made;
We will rejoice and be glad in it.

PSALM 118:24 NKJV

_____

_____

_____

_____

_____

_____

_____

_____

_____

_____

_____

_____

_____

_____

_____

_____

_____

_____

_____

_____

It's no use to grumble and complain; it's just
as cheap and easy to rejoice; when God sorts
out the weather and sends rain—why, rain's
my choice. —James Whitcomb Riley

Whether you eat or drink or whatever you do,
do it all for the glory of God.

1 CORINTHIANS 10:31 NIV

_____

_____

_____

_____

_____

_____

_____

_____

_____

_____

_____

_____

_____

_____

_____

_____

_____

_____

*If we have the ability to travel for pleasure,
we are privileged—even if our lodgings are
solely economy and our meals are ordered
at a drive-thru window. Any vacation we take
is a gift. Let's open it with gratitude
and enjoy it to the fullest.*

I remember what happened long ago;
I consider everything you have done.
I think about all you have made.

PSALM 143:5 NCV

You are never too old to set another goal or
dream a new dream. C.S. Lewis

Warn those who are lazy, comfort those who are frightened, take tender care of those who are weak, and be patient with everyone. See that no one pays back evil for evil, but always try to do good to each other and to everyone else.

1 THESSALONIANS 5:14-15 TLB

_____
_____
_____
_____
_____
_____
_____
_____
_____
_____
_____
_____
_____
_____
_____
_____
_____
_____

Do all the good you can, by all the means you can, in all the ways you can, in all the places you can, at all the times you can, to all the people you can, as long as ever you can.
—John Wesley

Ever since the world was created, people have seen the earth and sky. Through everything God made, they can clearly see his invisible qualities—his eternal power and divine nature. So they have no excuse for not knowing God.

ROMANS 1:20 NLT

Every person in a crowd is a story being written one moment at a time.

Our citizenship is in heaven.

PHILIPPIANS 3:20 NIV

_____

_____

_____

_____

_____

_____

_____

_____

_____

_____

_____

_____

_____

_____

_____

_____

_____

_____

_____

_____

_____

_____

_____

_By choosing to super-size our love and travel-
size our possessions, we can make the most
of the time we have here on earth and leave
behind a legacy of incomparable worth._

"Take your sandals off your feet, for the place on which you are standing is holy ground."

EXODUS 3:5 ESV

_____

_____

_____

_____

_____

_____

_____

_____

_____

_____

_____

_____

_____

_____

_____

_____

_____

_____

_____

_____

_____

_____

_____

_____

_____

_____

_____

_____

_____

_____

_____

_____

_____

_____

_____

_____

We may never see a burning bush in Central Park, but we may become more aware of God's whisper when the wind blows through the trees over our heads, or of God's loving care for all he's made when we delight in a blanket of wildflowers beneath our feet. The more aware we are of God's presence with us at all times, the more tempted we may be to take off our shoes.

We should love people not only with words and talk,
but by our actions and true caring.

1 JOHN 3:18 NCV

_____

_____

_____

_____

_____

_____

_____

_____

_____

_____

_____

_____

_____

_____

_____

_____

_____

_____

_____

_____

_____

_____

Making friends while we're making memories—even if we never understand a word the other person says—makes every journey a more enjoyable one.

Like cold water to a weary soul
is good news from a distant land.

PROVERBS 25:25 NIV

_____

_____

_____

_____

_____

_____

_____

_____

_____

_____

_____

_____

_____

_____

_____

_____

_____

_____

_____

_____

_____

_____

_____

_____

_____

_____

_____

_____

_____

_____

_____

_____

_____

_____

_____

_____

_____

_____

_____

_____

*What if the point of our travels is not in
seeing how the world changes us, but in how
our presence changes the world?*

"I am leaving you with a gift—peace of mind and heart. And the peace I give is a gift the world cannot give. So don't be troubled or afraid."

JOHN 14:27 NLT

_____

_____

_____

_____

_____

_____

_____

_____

_____

_____

_____

_____

_____

_____

_____

_____

_____

_____

_____

God cannot give us happiness and peace apart from Himself because it is not there. There is no such thing. —C.S. Lewis

Blessed are those whose strength is in you,
whose hearts are set on pilgrimage.

PSALM 84:5 NIV

_____

_____

_____

_____

_____

_____

_____

_____

_____

_____

_____

_____

_____

_____

_____

_____

_____

_____

_____

_____

If all the world is sacred—because there's not a corner where God's presence isn't found—then any journey can be a pilgrimage and every traveler a pilgrim.

You see me when I travel
and when I rest at home.
You know everything I do.

PSALM 139:3 NLT

_____
_____
_____
_____
_____
_____
_____
_____
_____
_____
_____
_____
_____
_____
_____
_____
_____
_____
_____

Delight in every unexpected joy
God brings your way.

Let all that I am praise the LORD;
may I never forget the good things he does for me.

PSALM 103:2 NLT

_____

_____

_____

_____

_____

_____

_____

_____

_____

_____

_____

_____

_____

_____

_____

_____

_____

_____

_____

_____

Let's do more than count our blessings. Let's make our blessings count. The more we take time to celebrate the gifts we've been given, the more grateful we'll feel.

"Do not fear, for I am with you;
Do not anxiously look about you, for I am your God.
I will strengthen you, surely I will help you."

ISAIAH 41:10 NASB

_____

_____

_____

_____

_____

_____

_____

_____

_____

_____

_____

_____

_____

_____

_____

_____

_____

_____

_____

_____

_____

_____

_____

_____

_____

_____

_____

_____

_____

_____

_____

_____

_____

_____

_____

_____

_____

_____

_____

_____

*To reconnect with God, you first have to
disconnect—turn off your phone and power
down your computer. Plug yourself in to the
ultimate power source. It's a great way to
recharge from the inside out.*

Those who live in the shelter of the Most High
will find rest in the shadow of the Almighty.
This I declare about the LORD:
He alone is my refuge, my place of safety;
he is my God, and I trust him.

PSALM 91:1-2 NLT

The more aware we are of God's presence
wherever we go, the more opportunities for
growth we'll find open up to us along the way.

Sketch or attach a photo of a favorite place or memory.

The LORD will keep you from all harm—
he will watch over your life;
the LORD will watch over your coming and going
both now and forevermore.

PSALM 121:7-8 NIV

_____
_____
_____
_____
_____
_____
_____
_____
_____
_____
_____
_____
_____
_____
_____
_____
_____
_____
_____
_____
_____
_____
_____
_____
_____

_____

_____

_____

_____

_____

_____

_____

_____

_____

_____

_____

_____

_____

_____

_____

_____

_____

*We can find great joy in the nostalgia of
what's familiar, but we need to add to our
store of memories and not try to survive
on a life of reruns.*

The heavens are yours; the earth also is yours;
the world and all that is in it, you have founded them.

PSALM 89:11 ESV

_____

_____

_____

_____

_____

_____

_____

_____

_____

_____

_____

_____

_____

_____

_____

_____

_____

_____

_____

_____

_____

It's better to see something once than
to hear about it a thousand times.

> "I am the one who made the earth
> and created people to live on it.
> With my hands I stretched out the heavens.
> All the stars are at my command."
>
> ISAIAH 45:12 NLT

_____

_____

_____

_____

_____

_____

_____

_____

_____

_____

_____

_____

_____

_____

_____

_____

_____

_____

_____

The real voyage of discovery consists
not in seeking new landscapes,
but in having new eyes. –Marcel Proust

"With my great strength and powerful arm I made the earth and all its people and every animal. I can give these things of mine to anyone I choose."

JEREMIAH 27:5 NLT

_____

_____

_____

_____

_____

_____

_____

_____

_____

_____

_____

_____

_____

_____

_____

_____

_____

_____

_____

Travel is the only thing you buy
that makes you richer.

"You are worthy, our Lord and God, to receive glory and honor and power, for you created all things, and by your will they were created and have their being."

REVELATION 4:11 NIV

_____

_____

_____

_____

_____

_____

_____

_____

_____

_____

_____

_____

_____

_____

_____

_____

_____

_____

_____

_____

_____

_____

_____

_____

_____

_____

_____

_____

_____

_____

_____

_____

_____

_____

_____

_____

_____

_____

_____

The world is not a checklist of things to see and do that we can cross off in one lifetime. It's a curiosity shop, so filled with mysterious treasures that every time we take another look, we discover something new.

Who has measured the waters in the hollow of his hand and marked off the heavens with a span, enclosed the dust of the earth in a measure and weighed the mountains in scales and the hills in a balance?

ISAIAH 40:12 ESV

_____

_____

_____

_____

_____

_____

_____

_____

_____

_____

_____

_____

_____

_____

_____

_____

_____

_____

_____

_____

_____

_____

You can't see the whole sky
through a bamboo tube.

Praise him, sun and moon;
praise him, all you shining stars.
Praise him, you highest heavens
and you waters above the skies.

PSALM 148:3-5 NIV

_____

_____

_____

_____

_____

_____

_____

_____

_____

_____

_____

_____

_____

_____

_____

_____

_____

_____

_____

_____

_____

_____

_____

Return to your favorite place, but don't forget
to pack a fresh point of view.

Who gives the sun for light by day
And the fixed order of the moon and the stars for light by night,
Who stirs up the sea so that its waves roar;
The LORD of hosts is His name.

JEREMIAH 31:35 NASB

_____

_____

_____

_____

_____

_____

_____

_____

_____

_____

_____

_____

_____

_____

_____

_____

_____

_____

_____

_____

Travel broadens the mind.

He himself gives everyone life and breath and everything else.
From one man he made all the nations, that they should inhabit
the whole earth; and he marked out their appointed times in history
and the boundaries of their lands.

ACTS 17:25-26 NIV

_____

_____

_____

_____

_____

_____

_____

_____

_____

_____

_____

_____

_____

_____

_____

_____

_____

_____

_____

Do not let your happiness depend on something you may lose. -C.S. Lewis

Through him all things were made;
without him nothing was made that has been made

JOHN 1:3 NIV

_____

_____

_____

_____

_____

_____

_____

_____

_____

_____

_____

_____

_____

_____

_____

_____

_____

_____

_____

_____

Unless we learn to cherish **home**, and the
beauty of an ordinary day, we may wind up
believing that the best part of life is our next
big trip to somewhere else. If we do, we'll miss
what's right in front of us: the adventure
waiting at our own front door.

The life of every living thing is in his hand,
and the breath of every human being.

JOB 12:10 NLT

_____

_____

_____

_____

_____

_____

_____

_____

_____

_____

_____

_____

_____

_____

_____

_____

_____

_____

_____

_____

No exotic location could ever provide the joy we find in the presence of those we love.

Let the heavens be glad, and the earth rejoice!
Let the sea and everything in it shout his praise!
Let the fields and their crops burst out with joy!
Let the trees of the forest rustle with praise
before the LORD, for he is coming!

PSALM 96:11-13 NLT

_____

_____

_____

_____

_____

_____

_____

_____

_____

_____

_____

_____

_____

_____

_____

_____

_____

_____

_For in the true nature of things, if we rightly
consider, every green tree is far more glorious
than if it were made of gold and silver._
                                    —Martin Luther

In whose hand are the depths of the earth,
The peaks of the mountains are His also.
Come, let us worship and bow down,
Let us kneel before the LORD our Maker.

PSALM 95:4,6 NASB

If the visible world is so immense and complex that we can never fully comprehend it, surely the invisible world is even more so.

LORD, you have made many things;
with your wisdom you made them all.
The earth is full of your riches.

PSALM 104:24 NCV

_____

_____

_____

_____

_____

_____

_____

_____

_____

_____

_____

_____

_____

_____

_____

_____

_____

_____

_____

_____

_____

_____

_____

A vacation is not just a destination.
It includes a journey.
We can't travel without moving!

He loves righteousness and justice;
The earth is full of the goodness of the LORD.

PSALM 33:5 NKJV

_____

_____

_____

_____

_____

_____

_____

_____

_____

_____

_____

_____

_____

_____

_____

_____

_____

_____

*When our vacation is centered around
the people we love, what we do and where
we go doesn't matter as much. Love can
be tricky and messy, but it can also
be the deepest, richest part of our lives.*

God has given them a desire to know the future. He does everything just right and on time, but people can never completely understand what he is doing.

ECCLESIASTES 3:11 NCV

_____

_____

_____

_____

_____

_____

_____

_____

_____

_____

_____

_____

_____

_____

_____

_____

_____

_____

_____

_____

_____

_____

_____

_____

_____

_____

_____

_____

_____

_____

_____

_____

_____

_____

_____

_____

_____

_____

_____

_____

_____

*Expect the best, pack for the worst,
and prepare to make some unexpected
memories along the way.*

"You shall go out in joy,
and be led back in peace;
the mountains and the hills before you
shall burst into song,
and all the trees of the field shall clap their hands."

ISAIAH 55:12 NRSV

_____

_____

_____

_____

_____

_____

_____

_____

_____

_____

_____

_____

_____

_____

_____

_____

_____

_____

_____

_____

It is good to have an end to journey toward;
but it is the journey that matters, in the end.
-Ernest Hemingway

"You alone are the LORD. You made the heavens, even the highest heavens, and all their starry host, the earth and all that is on it, the seas and all that is in them."

NEHEMIAH 9:6 NIV

_____

_____

_____

_____

_____

_____

_____

_____

_____

_____

_____

_____

_____

_____

_____

_____

_____

_____

_____

*Imagine every image you take as a thank-
you postcard to God. Not only will you find a
unique way to spend more time interacting
with your heavenly Father, you'll also find
your inner well of gratitude overflowing
more regularly.*

Long ago you laid the foundation of the earth
and made the heavens with your hands.

PSALM 102:25 NLT

Stay curious: keep asking questions,
exploring new places, and being humbled
by the fact that there's always more to learn.

The LORD is my shepherd; I shall not want.
He makes me lie down in green pastures.
He leads me beside still waters.
He restores my soul.

PSALM 23:2-3 ESV

_____
_____
_____
_____
_____
_____
_____
_____
_____
_____
_____
_____
_____
_____
_____
_____
_____
_____
_____

Travel can challenge and delight us. It can open our eyes, stretch our minds, and charm our hearts. But it can also make us appreciate the quiet pleasures of home.

When I consider your heavens, the work of your fingers,
the moon and the stars, which you have set in place,
what is mankind that you are mindful of them,
human beings that you care for them?

PSALM 8:3-4 NIV

_____

_____

_____

_____

_____

_____

_____

_____

_____

_____

_____

_____

_____

_____

_____

_____

_____

_____

_____

_____

_____

_____

_____

_____

_____

_____

_____

_____

_____

_____

_____

_____

_____

_____

_____

_____

_____

_____

_____

_____

Just say no to boredom. Nurture curiosity
instead of apathy. You don't have to stop
exploring—even if you never journey
far from home.

The LORD directs the steps of the godly.
He delights in every detail of their lives.

PSALM 37:23 NLT

_____

_____

_____

_____

_____

_____

_____

_____

_____

_____

_____

_____

_____

_____

_____

_____

_____

_____

_____

_____

_____

Choosing to use free time in a way that refreshes the soul is a wise choice. Let's just be certain it's still a choice and not a habit.

Trust in the LORD with all your heart;
do not depend on your own understanding.
Seek his will in all you do,
and he will show you which path to take.

PROVERBS 3:5-6 NLT

_____

_____

_____

_____

_____

_____

_____

_____

_____

_____

_____

_____

_____

_____

_____

_____

_____

_____

Life is a journey that keeps moving forward.

> "Yours, O LORD, is the greatness and the power and the glory and the victory and the majesty, for all that is in the heavens and in the earth is yours."

1 CHRONICLES 29:11 ESV

_____

_____

_____

_____

_____

_____

_____

_____

_____

_____

_____

_____

_____

_____

_____

_____

_____

_____

_____

_____

_____

_____

_____

_____

_____

_____

_____

_____

_____

_____

_____

_____

_____

_____

_____

_____

_____

_____

_____

_____

_____

*Whether we're on the road, or safe at home,
putting God's will before our own reminds us
who is actually in control at all times.*

> "My Presence will go with you, and I will give you rest."
>
> EXODUS 33:14 NIV

_____

_____

_____

_____

_____

_____

_____

_____

_____

_____

_____

_____

_____

_____

_____

_____

_____

_____

Listen for what God has to say to you in the spaces between activities, when you're quiet enough to hear his voice.

"I will never fail you. I will never abandon you."

HEBREWS 13:5 NLT

_____

_____

_____

_____

_____

_____

_____

_____

_____

_____

_____

_____

_____

_____

_____

_____

_____

_____

_____

_____

_____

_____

From the miracle of birth to the laws of gravity, the world God created is wonder piled upon wonder.

The LORD is near to all who call upon Him,
To all who call upon Him in truth.

PSALM 145:18 NKJV

_____

_____

_____

_____

_____

_____

_____

_____

_____

_____

_____

_____

_____

_____

_____

_____

_____

_____

_____

_____

_____

_____

_____

_____

_____

_____

_____

_____

_____

_____

_____

_____

_____

_____

_____

_____

_____

_____

_____

_____

_____

_____

_____

_____

_____

Make the most of the time spent in the company of those you love. They are always worth the journey.

"His purpose was for the nations to seek after God and perhaps feel their way toward him and find him— though he is not far from any one of us."

ACTS 17:27 NLT

Jesus is God spelling himself out in language
humanity can understand. —S.D. Gordon

Sketch or attach a photo of a favorite place or memory.

"The LORD your God is with you;
the mighty One will save you.
He will rejoice over you.
You will rest in his love;
he will sing and be joyful about you."

ZEPHANIAH 3:17 NCV

Asking God to join us on our journey
helps make us more aware of his presence
at every turn.

Your word is like a lamp for my feet
and a light for my path.

PSALM 119:105 NCV

_____

_____

_____

_____

_____

_____

_____

_____

_____

_____

_____

_____

_____

_____

_____

_____

_____

_____

_____

_____

At heart, each and every one of us is a lost pilgrim searching for the road home. We're all in need of a knowledgeable guide to help us navigate the twists and turns of life.

These commandments that I give you today are to be on your hearts....
Talk about them when you sit at home and when you walk along the
road, when you lie down and when you get up.

DEUTERONOMY 6:6-7 NIV

_____

_____

_____

_____

_____

_____

_____

_____

_____

_____

_____

_____

_____

_____

_____

_____

_____

_____

_____

_____

_____

_____

_____

*Wherever we go, we go with God. May every
journey you take, and memory you make,
help you become more aware of his power, his
presence, and his love.*